Thank You, You, *Lord*

A Creative Gratitude Journal

BARBOUR BOOKS

An Imprint of Barbour Publishing, Inc.

Published by Barbour Books, an imprint of Barbour Publishing, 1810 Barbour Drive, Uhrichsville, Ohio 44683, www.barbourbooks.com

Our mission is to inspire the world with the life-changing message of the Bible.

Member of the
Evangelical Christian
Publishers Association

Printed in China.

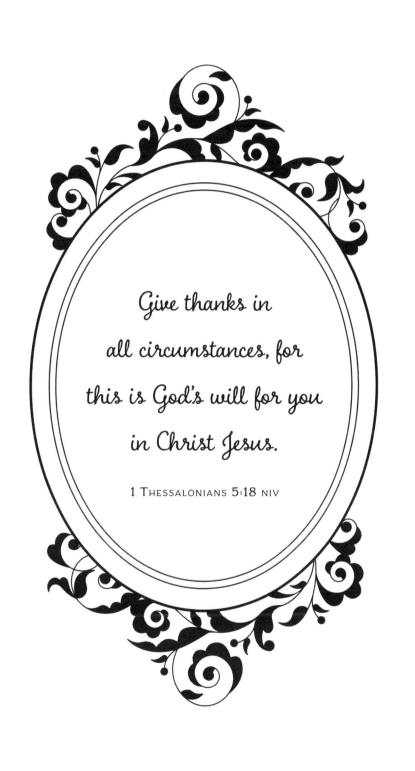

Give thanks in
all circumstances, for
this is God's will for you
in Christ Jesus.

1 THESSALONIANS 5:18 NIV

What do you have to be thankful for? List your top five.

Dear God, make me appreciative of all the wonderful gifts You give.
When I take things for granted, show me the error of my ways. Fill my mind
and heart with gratitude for the many blessings I have. Amen.

....
....
....
....
....
....
....
....
....
....
....
....
....
....
....
....
....
....
....
....

This is the day which the LORD hath made;
we will rejoice and be glad in it.

PSALM 118:24 KJV

Each new day is full of potential.
What are you looking forward to seeing God do today?

....
....
....
....
....
....
....
....
....
....
....
....
....
....
....
....
....
....
....
....
....
....
....
....
....

Let me appreciate the gift of this day, Lord.
Help me to use my time wisely, teach me to rejoice,
and fill me with joy that never ends. Amen.

....
....
....
....
....
....
....
....
....
....
....
....
....
....
....
....
....
....

Since everything God created is good, we should
not reject any of it but receive it with thanks.

1 TIMOTHY 4:4 NLT

What have you allowed to annoy you lately, and how can you turn that around to see the good God has placed in it?

....

....

....

....

....

....

....

....

....

....

....

....

....

....

....

....

....

....

....

....

....

....

....

....

....

....

Like a bee buzzing around a picnic table, whose beauty and purpose is in pollination and making honey, Lord, help me see good in the things of life that tend to annoy and frustrate me. For all You give has value, and we praise You as Creator. Amen.

The LORD directs the steps of the godly.
He delights in every detail of their lives.

PSALM 37:23 NLT

God works His wonders even in the small stuff.
What are some of the small details you've seen God bless today?

Thank You, Lord, for caring about the small things—from my missing
keys to the availability of my favorite ice cream. Your hand
in the little details of life makes me feel loved. Amen.

The day is thine, the night also is thine:
thou hast prepared the light and the sun.

PSALM 74:16 KJV

As the day comes to a close, what do you want to thank God for?

Heavenly Father, another day is done. Thank You
for the things I accomplished today with Your help,
and thank You for abiding with me as I sleep. Amen.

A man hath joy by the answer of his mouth:
and a word spoken in due season, how good is it!

Proverbs 15:23 KJV

Who has spoken words of comfort and joy into your life lately?

Dear Lord, thank You for those whose words bless my heart.
May I do likewise to spread kindness not only through
my words, but also with my actions. Amen.

A wise man will hear, and will increase learning; and a man of understanding shall attain unto wise counsels.

PROVERBS 1:5 KJV

What is the best advice you ever received?

Thank You, Lord, for thoughtful words of wisdom
shared in such a way that I can use them in my life.
May I always appreciate advice kindly given. Amen.

One person gives freely, yet gains even more;
another withholds unduly, but comes to poverty.

PROVERBS 11:24 NIV

What has God given you that is meant to be shared?

Take what I have, Lord, and use it for Your glory. I have nothing except what You have given me. Help me to share from my abundance and to give all that I can to those who are in need. Amen.

....

....

....

....

....

....

....

....

....

....

....

....

....

....

....

I know that nothing is better for them than to rejoice, and to do good in their lives, and also that every man should eat and drink and enjoy the good of all his labor—it is the gift of God.

ECCLESIASTES 3:12–13 NKJV

In what ways do you enjoy life to its fullest?

This world You have created, Lord, is miraculous and beautiful, and I thank You for all the ways You allow me to enjoy it to the utmost. May I never stop appreciating its beauty. Amen.

....
....
....
....
....
....
....
....
....
....
....
....
....
....
....
....
....
....
....
....
....

I know whom I have believed, and am convinced that he is able to guard what I have entrusted to him until that day.

2 TIMOTHY 1:12 NIV

What is your personal statement of faith?

Lord, I am so grateful to know You—and I am learning more about Your character every day. You are holy and sovereign and righteous and just. You are loving and faithful and always good. I thank You, my Lord. Amen.

By the word of the LORD were the heavens made;
and all the host of them by the breath of his mouth.

PSALM 33:6 KJV

What is the most amazing part of creation you have seen?

Creator, Your imagination has yielded wonders beyond comprehension. We stand in awe before Your mighty power. Thank You for finding a place in all of this for me. Your love shines forth throughout all of Your creation. Praise be unto You! Amen.

He spreads the snow like wool and scatters the frost like ashes.
He hurls down his hail like pebbles. Who can withstand
his icy blast? He sends his word and melts them;
he stirs up his breezes, and the waters flow.

PSALM 147:16–18 NIV

What is your favorite part of winter?

Dear Jesus, thank You for another season come and gone. I am in awe of the careful way You craft one day to the next in a seamless array of beauty and splendor. Help me to recognize and appreciate the unique gifts each season has to offer. Amen.

He that dwelleth in the secret place of the most
High shall abide under the shadow the Almighty.

Psalm 91:1 kjv

Where is your secret place to be alone with God?

I see Thy mercy, limitless as space,
I see Thy love and feel Thy close embrace;
And though Thy presence fills the universe,
Yet close as hands and heart Thou art to me.
-OLGA J. WEISS

How sweet are thy words unto my taste!
yea, sweeter than honey to my mouth!

PSALM 119:103 KJV

What favorite scripture brings you joy?

Your Holy Word is living and comforting. Your amazing promises bring joy and life that get me through each day. Thank You for Your living words. Amen.

....

....

....

....

....

....

....

....

....

....

....

....

....

....

....

....

....

....

....

....

The LORD is nigh unto them that are of a broken heart;
and saveth such as be of a contrite spirit.

PSALM 34:18 KJV

What mistakes have you laid at Jesus' feet?

Lord, cleanse my mind of unworthy things I've seen, heard, and read that have filled my mind with confused, idle thoughts. Remove what I've let build up bit by bit. Help me refocus on only what is pure, lovely, and right in Your eyes. Amen.

"Forget the former things; do not dwell on the past. See, I am doing a new thing! Now it springs up; do you not perceive it? I am making a way in the wilderness and streams in the wasteland."

ISAIAH 43:18–19 NIV

What is something new that you are looking forward to?

Thank You for giving me this thing to look forward to, Father. I'm so excited that I can hardly wait! Help me to recognize the little joys in each moment of my life so I will look forward to living each and every second of the day with hope and enthusiasm. Amen.

....
....
....
....
....
....
....
....
....
....
....
....
....
....
....
....
....
....
....

Therefore be patient, brethren, until the coming of the Lord. See how the farmer waits for the precious fruit of the earth, waiting patiently for it until it receives the early and latter rain. You also be patient. Establish your hearts, for the coming of the Lord is at hand.

JAMES 5:7–8 NKJV

What have you been waiting for that has tested your patience?

Lord, help me to wait in patience so I don't miss the goodness
You want to bestow. Remind me that my anxiety will not hurry
Your will along and will not bring me comfort. Amen.

So we thy people and sheep of thy pasture will give thee thanks for ever: we will shew forth thy praise to all generations.

PSALM 79:13 KJV

What are you most thankful for today?

For all the blessings of the year,
For all the friends we hold so dear,
For peace on earth, both far and near,
We thank Thee, Lord.
For life and health, those common things,
Which every day and hour brings,
For home, where our affection clings,
We thank Thee, Lord.
For love of Thine, which never tires,
Which all our better thought inspires,
And warms our lives with heavenly fires,
We thank Thee, Lord.

-ALBERT H. HUTCHINSON

For lo, the winter is past, the rain is over and gone.
The flowers appear on the earth; the time of singing has come,
and the voice of the turtledove is heard in our land.

SONG OF SOLOMON 2:11–12 NKJV

What is your favorite part of the spring season?

Lord, I thank You for the promise of spring. For the trees and flowers that open their buds. For the babies among the animals. I treasure each sign of new life as a reminder of the new life You provide for us. Amen.

Don't worry about anything; instead, pray about everything. Tell God what you need, and thank him for all he has done.

PHILIPPIANS 4:6 NLT

What worries are you ready to place in God's hands?

Lord, thank You for being available 24-7—when I'm in
trouble, when I need a friend, when I feel like praising
You, and when I just want to say hello to my Father. Amen.

So that we may boldly say, The Lord is my helper,
and I will not fear what man shall do unto me.

HEBREWS 13:6 KJV

How has God shown you that He is watching over you?

Lord, if You withdraw Your hand, there is no grace.
If You cease to guide us, we have no wisdom.
If You no longer defend us, we have no courage.
If You do not strengthen us, our chastity is vulnerable.
If You do not keep a holy watch over us,
our watchfulness cannot protect us.
By ourselves we sink, we perish;
when You are with us, we are uplifted, we live.
We are shaky, You make us firm.
We are lukewarm, You inflame us.

—Thomas à Kempis

One who has unreliable friends soon comes to ruin,
but there is a friend who sticks closer than a brother.

PROVERBS 18:24 NIV

Who is the friend you are most grateful for and why?

Lord, I thank You for my wonderful friends! As I think about the treasure chest of my close friends, casual friends, and acquaintances, I am grateful for the blessings and the joys each one brings to my life. May I always be a worthy friend in return. Amen.

They that sow in tears shall reap in joy.

PSALM 126:5 KJV

What joy have you found after coming through your greatest sorrow?

Dear Lord, take up the tangled strands, where we have wrought in vain,
that by the skill of Thy dear hands some beauty may remain.

–Mrs. F. G. Burroughs

Until now you have not asked for anything in my name.
Ask and you will receive, and your joy will be complete.

JOHN 16:24 NIV

How do you know God answers prayer?

*Lord, I thank You for the joy of answered prayer! I delight in
You and thank You with a full heart. I asked, and You answered.
I receive what You give with a grateful heart. Amen.*

A father of the fatherless, a defender
of widows, is God in His holy habitation.

PSALM 68:5 NKJV

How has God shown Himself to be the best type of father in your life?

....

....

....

....

....

....

....

....

....

....

....

....

....

....

....

....

....

....

....

....

....

....

....

....

....

*Dear Heavenly Father, I thank You for taking me in as one of
Your children. Your love is unconditional and Your patience enduring.
Forgive me for the times when I am less than You created me to be.
Help me to grow and mature and develop into Your image. Amen.*

Draw nigh to God, and he will draw nigh to you.

James 4:8 kjv

How has God comforted you when you've been lonely?

....
....
....
....
....
....
....
....
....
....
....
....
....
....
....
....
....
....
....
....
....
....

*Father, I thank You that wherever I go, whether
alone in hiding or in the middle of a crowded room,
You are with me and will never leave me. Amen.*

*And the Lord direct your hearts into the love of God,
and into the patient waiting for Christ.*

2 THESSALONIANS 3:5 KJV

How has waiting taught you to trust in God's timing?

Lord, I thank You for the seasons of waiting. For even when I can't see things happening, I know You are working on my behalf. Help me to always appreciate these times of stillness. Amen.

I was glad when they said unto me,
Let us go into the house of the LORD.

PSALM 122:1 KJV

Where do you meet with other Christians to worship God?

Lord, I thank You for a group of Christians to gather with in a place of worship where we can focus on You and Your great gifts. May we always value this special time together. Amen.

....

....

....

....

....

....

....

....

....

....

....

....

....

The LORD hath appeared of old unto me, saying,
Yea, I have loved thee with an everlasting love:
therefore with lovingkindness have I drawn thee.

JEREMIAH 31:3 KJV

Do you realize how much the God of creation loves you?

Who am I, Lord, that You take notice of me? I cannot believe that You love me the way You do. Though I don't understand, I do accept Your gracious love, and I am thankful from the depths of my soul. Amen.

*Blessed be the Lord, who daily loadeth us
with benefits, even the God of our salvation.*

PSALM 68:19 KJV

When we ask God for our daily bread, what do we mean?

Lord, I do not even know what I need to be better than I am today,
but in Your wisdom, You see my every need. Give me what You will,
in order that I might honor and glorify You. Amen.

Hear me when I call, O God of my righteousness! You have relieved me in my distress; have mercy on me, and hear my prayer.

Psalm 4:1 NKJV

When and where do you spend time alone talking with God?

I know You are listening, Lord, for when I take my jumbled thoughts and start to focus on You, my heart rate calms and things start to become clearer in my mind. Even though I may not know Your answer now, I know You have heard my cries and will show me what I need to do. You always do. Amen.

God sets the solitary in families.

PSALM 68:6 NKJV

Who is the family member you are closest to and why?

....

....

....

....

....

....

....

....

....

....

....

....

....

....

....

....

....

....

....

....

....

....

....

....

....

....

I thank You, Lord, for my family members. Each of them
is special and important to my life in their own way.
Help me not to take any of them for granted. Amen.

*Be kindly affectioned one to another with brotherly love;
in honour preferring one another.*

ROMANS 12:10 KJV

How can you be a blessing to others?

Lord, help me show love to others, so they know I belong to You. Amen.

Let another man praise you, and not your own mouth;
a stranger, and not your own lips.

Proverbs 27:2 NKJV

What words of praise have you received from someone else. . . words that have been an encouragement to you?

Thank You, Lord, for people who speak words of encouragement into my life and help me see my worth. May I also be a person who speaks words of praise over others so they see the beauty You have planted in their lives. Amen.

Share with the Lord's people who are in need.
Practice hospitality.

ROMANS 12:13 NIV

How do you enjoy showing hospitality?

Lord, I thank You for my home. Show my heart opportunities to open this home to others. I want to share what You've provided for me. I am grateful that Your Spirit is present here. Give me a generous, open heart, and use my home for Your good purposes. Amen.

"You are worthy, our Lord and God, to receive
glory and honor and power, for you created all things,
and by your will they were created and have their being."

REVELATION 4:11 NIV

How do you stay present in each moment, appreciating each day God gives?

....

....

....

....

....

....

....

....

....

....

....

....

....

....

....

....

....

....

....

....

....

....

....

....

....

*Help me not to rush ahead of You, Lord. I have lessons to learn
at each stage of life. Help me to slow down so that the lessons
can take root. And I will give You praise. Amen.*

The earth is the LORD's, and the fulness thereof;
the world, and they that dwell therein.

PSALM 24:1 KJV

What part of creation has God placed under your care?

Lord, I thank You for all You have created. Please make me a wise steward of all living things. Help me to build up, rather than destroy. Inspire me to share, to give, and to love. Amen.

Build ye houses, and dwell in them;
and plant gardens, and eat the fruit of them.

JEREMIAH 29:5 KJV

What do you love about the place where you live?

Dear Lord, I'm so grateful for a place to live. It may not be perfect, but it is home, and I am blessed. Help me remember those who have no roof to cover their heads. Amen.

When you have eaten and are satisfied, praise the
LORD your God for the good land he has given you.

DEUTERONOMY 8:10 NIV

What is your favorite food?

Thank You, Lord, for each meal cooked by loving hands.
I am truly blessed to have food on my plate. Please use its
nourishment to strengthen my body to do Your will. Amen.

Give thanks to the LORD, for he is good;
his love endures forever.

1 CHRONICLES 16:34 NIV

Why should we give thanks to the Lord?

*Dear Lord, there is so much to be thankful for. Not just for
the things that please me but also for the times You have said
"no" or "wait." For I can see Your love for me in all things. Amen.*

Honour the LORD with thy substance, and with the firstfruits
of all thine increase: so shall thy barns be filled with plenty,
and thy presses shall burst out with new wine.

PROVERBS 3:9–10 KJV

What is something you have been blessed with that you too often take for granted?

Oh Father, soften my heart toward those who are less fortunate
than I am. Help me to appreciate the blessings I have been
given and to share from my abundance with others. Amen.

A merry heart maketh a cheerful countenance.

Proverbs 15:13 KJV

What have you laughed about lately?

Fill my heart with Your joy, Lord. Change the light of my countenance to happiness so that everyone will know the effect You have had on my life. I praise You for Your gracious gift. Amen.

The LORD is my strength and my shield;
my heart trusts in him, and he helps me.

PSALM 28:7 NIV

Who do you know and pray for who is serving in the military?

Lord, I thank You for all the men and women serving in our armed forces. They choose to put their lives on the line so we can have freedom and peace—and for that I am truly grateful. Protect them, and keep them safe. Comfort them, and give them strength when they are away from loved ones. Bless too the families who send soldiers to war or for duty overseas. I pray that You would meet their every need, Lord. Amen.

In peace I will lie down and sleep,
for you alone, O LORD, will keep me safe.

PSALM 4:8 NLT

When do you feel most at peace?

*Thank You, Father, for the gift of peace and stillness. How often
I take it for granted! Help me to discover You in every quiet
moment—to listen carefully to Your gentle voice. Amen.*

"At the right time, I, the LORD, will make it happen."

ISAIAH 60:22 NLT

What is something you have been looking forward to happening?

*Lord, I thank You for things to come and the hope we have that
You already know the future. Please guide me to do Your will
so that I can rejoice in the outcome of each day. Amen.*

Thy word is a lamp unto my feet,
and a light unto my path.

Psalm 119:105 KJV

What is your favorite scripture?

I love Your Word, Lord. Thank You for giving us the
holy scriptures to direct our paths. I will meditate
on them daily as I seek to fulfill Your will. Amen.

I am reminded of your sincere faith, which first
lived in your grandmother Lois and in your mother
Eunice and, I am persuaded, now lives in you also.

2 TIMOTHY 1:5 NIV

What are your mother's best qualities that you hope to have also?

....

....

....

....

....

....

....

....

....

....

....

....

....

....

....

....

....

....

....

....

....

....

....

....

Lord, thank You for godly mothers. Thank You for the women You have put in my life to give me wise counsel. May I be wise to listen, and may I bring them joy. Amen.

Then the LORD God said, "It is not good for the man to be alone. I will make a helper who is just right for him." So the LORD God formed from the ground all the wild animals and all the birds of the sky. He brought them to the man to see what he would call them, and the man chose a name for each one.

GENESIS 2:18–19 NLT

Do you have a pet? If so, how does your pet bring you joy and comfort?

*Thank You, Lord, for animals we can have as pets. I am blessed
to know You as Creator better through these creatures'
unconditional love and sweet companionship. Amen.*

You have set all the borders of the earth;
You have made summer and winter.

PSALM 74:17 NKJV

What is your favorite part of summer?

Lord, thank You for the simple pleasures of summer: a pleasant evening outdoors and delicious food to share with friends and family. I am so grateful for Your everyday gifts that bring my loved ones together. Amen.

"Say to him: 'Long life to you! Good health to you and your household! And good health to all that is yours!' "

1 SAMUEL 25:6 NIV

In what ways are you grateful for the health you have?

Lord, I thank You for my good health. It is a blessing. I pray for Your power to sustain me as I take care of myself each day and as I face challenges that will come with old age. Amen.

O come, let us sing unto the LORD: let us make a joyful noise to the rock of our salvation.

PSALM 95:1 KJV

What is a favorite song of praise you like to sing to the Lord?

I thank You, Lord, for music. Let the words of my mouth produce a joyful noise, acceptable and glorifying to You in all ways. Praise Your holy name! Amen.

Now to him who is able to do immeasurably more than all we ask or imagine, according to his power that is at work within us, to him be glory in the church and in Christ Jesus throughout all generations, for ever and ever! Amen.

EPHESIANS 3:20-21 NIV

How has God answered your prayers?

I praise You, Lord, for doing more than I'd even think of asking for. Amen.

The LORD also will be a refuge for the oppressed, a refuge in times of trouble.

PSALM 9:9 KJV

Where do you go to escape from the pressures of the world and talk to God?

Father, I sometimes need to escape: from the world, from myself, from the things that tie me down. Be my liberation and my sanctuary. Strengthen me for Your service. Amen.

Two are better than one, because they have a good return for their labor: If either of them falls down, one can help the other up. But pity anyone who falls and has no one to help them up.

ECCLESIASTES 4:9–10 NIV

Who are the friends you can most depend upon?

Thank You, Lord, for surrounding me with so many wonderful people who are supportive friends. I am grateful for the richness they bring to my life each day. Amen.

"Look at the birds of the air; they do not sow or reap or store away in barns, and yet your heavenly Father feeds them. Are you not much more valuable than they?"

MATTHEW 6:26 NIV

What do you enjoy about watching birds, and what do they teach you about God?

Thank You for Your amazing creations that fly and sing so sweetly throughout the day. Thank You for the lessons these creatures, from the smallest sparrow to the greatest eagle, have to teach us about trusting in You. Amen.

There hath no temptation taken you but such as is common to man: but God is faithful, who will not suffer you to be tempted above that ye are able; but will with the temptation also make a way to escape, that ye may be able to bear it.

1 CORINTHIANS 10:13 KJV

What temptations have you overcome lately?

*Lord, temptations seem to be all around me, but I understand that nothing
I face today is much different from what others have had to face.
Help me to remember that You will always stand beside me and give
me the strength to endure. And I will praise You for it. Amen.*

He administers justice for the fatherless and the widow,
and loves the stranger, giving him food and clothing.

DEUTERONOMY 10:18 NKJV

How can God use you to help another?

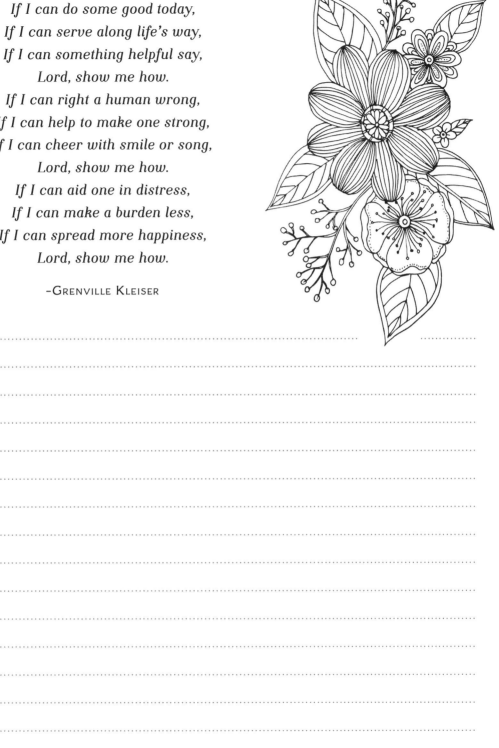

If I can do some good today,
If I can serve along life's way,
If I can something helpful say,
Lord, show me how.
If I can right a human wrong,
If I can help to make one strong,
If I can cheer with smile or song,
Lord, show me how.
If I can aid one in distress,
If I can make a burden less,
If I can spread more happiness,
Lord, show me how.

–GRENVILLE KLEISER

A gracious woman retaineth honour:
and strong men retain riches.

PROVERBS 11:16 KJV

What blessings has God bestowed on you that are greater than honor and riches?

....

....

....

....

....

....

....

....

....

....

....

....

....

....

....

....

....

....

....

....

....

....

....

....

*Lord, the blessings You bestow are immeasurable
and unending. May I be mindful to consider my
blessings each day and give You praise. Amen.*

A generous person will prosper;
whoever refreshes others will be refreshed.

PROVERBS 11:25 NIV

What act of kindness have you performed lately?

Lord, all that I have is from You. Help me to share with those You place in my path. Amen.

My child, eat honey, for it is good,
and the honeycomb is sweet to the taste.

PROVERBS 24:13 NLT

What is your favorite sweet treat?

I'm thankful, Lord, that You created sweet and yummy treats for us to eat. Help me to enjoy without overindulging in their delights. Nothing is sweeter than Your love! Amen.

The LORD is my strength and my shield;
my heart trusts in him, and he helps me.

PSALM 28:7 NIV

Have you been through a scary storm that God brought you through unscathed?

Father, thank You for the awesome power of Your creation. Though I may tremble in the face of storms, remind me that no storm lasts forever and that You are always cradling me securely in the palm of Your hand. Amen.

"I prayed for this child, and the LORD
has granted me what I asked of him."

1 SAMUEL 1:27 NIV

Is there a new baby in your circle of family and friends?
Describe the beauty of a new life just beginning.

Lord, I am humbled by this miracle of life. I am filled with hope
for the future and reminded of the new life You offer us all.
Thank You for this reminder of Your phenomenal love. Amen.

Come away, my beloved, and be like a gazelle
or like a young stag on the spice-laden mountains.

Song of Solomon 8:14 niv

What was your most memorable vacation?

Father, thank You for vacations! Thank You for blessing me with this opportunity to relax and gain perspective. Thank You for going with me when I step out of my regular routine. Help me to see You in a new and fresh way while I revel in Your glorious gift of rest. Amen.

You make known to me the path of life; you will fill me with joy in your presence, with eternal pleasures at your right hand.

PSALM 16:11 NIV

How have you seen God guiding you along the path of life?

There are times when I feel Your presence so strongly, Lord.
I know that You have orchestrated a masterpiece of which I am
a small but important part. Thank You for including me. Amen.

Jesus saith unto him, I am the way, the truth, and the life: no man cometh unto the Father, but by me.

JOHN 14:6 KJV

When did you decide to follow Jesus?

O Jesus, I have promised
To serve Thee to the end;
Be Thou forever near me,
My Master and my Friend;
I shall not fear the battle
If Thou art by my side,
Nor wander from the pathway
If Thou wilt be my Guide.

–JOHN E. BODE

To every thing there is a season,
and a time to every purpose under the heaven.

ECCLESIASTES 3:1 KJV

What is your favorite part of the fall season?

Even as the lively green of summer and the vibrant colors of early fall fade to drab brown, Lord, I see Your hand at work and praise the wonders of Your creation. Amen.

For the LORD is good; his mercy is everlasting;
and his truth endureth to all generations.

PSALM 100:5 KJV

How have you seen God's faithfulness in the generations of your family?

Lord, I thank You for people who have gone before me—family and friends—who have shown me what it means to walk in faith. Thank You for their righteous example. Amen.

I will both lay me down in peace, and sleep:
for thou, LORD, only makest me dwell in safety.

PSALM 4:8 KJV

What brings you the best feeling of rest?

Now the day is over,
Night is drawing nigh,
Shadows of the evening
Steal across the sky.
Jesus, give the weary
Calm and sweet repose;
With Thy tend'rest blessing
May our eyelids close.
When the morning waken
Then may I arise
Pure and fresh and sinless
In Thy holy eyes.

–SABINE BARING-GOULD